WHY YOUR VIDEO STRATEGY SUCKS

....

Thomas J Elliott

First Published by The Curious Film Company 2018

Copyright © 2018 Thomas J Elliott

ISBN-13: 978-1726110433

ISBN-10: 1726110435

Thomas J Elliott has asserted his right under the Copyright, Designs and Patents Act 1988 to be identified as the author of this work.

The information in this book is based on the author's experiences and opinions.

The publisher specifically disclaims responsibility for an adverse consequences, which may result from use of information contained herein.

Permission to use information has been sought by the authors.

Any breaches will be rectified in further editions of the book.

All rights reserved.

No part of this publication may be reproduced, stored in or introduced into a retrieval system, or transmitted in any form, or by any means (electronic, mechanical, photocopying, recording or otherwise) without the prior written permission of the author.

Any person who does any unauthorised act in relation to this publication may be liable to criminal prosecution and civil claims for damages.

Enquiries should be made to the publisher.

Cover image art by Thomas J Elliott - https://www.thomaselliottvisualcontent.com

Cover design by Thomas J Elliott - https://www.thomaselliottvisualcontent.com

Layout and typesetting: Thomas J Elliott.

DEDICATION

To those who inspired this book but are unlikely to read or learn from it…

I dedicate this book to you…

THANKS

A lot of people to thank for finally pushing me to get off my butt and write this fourth book:

My wife Zhifang and our daughter Zoey

My parents Catherine and John

Sam Rankin from Hightop Media

String Nguyen from Stringstory

Miguel Donnenfeld and Damien Blumenkranc from Creativa

Dominque Spanos

David Richardson

Brendan Black

Stephen Costan

Aleksi Vellis

John Carpenter

Mark Erder

Angela Cheung

The team at APV!

CONTENTS

INTRODUCTION:

About the author and about this book

CHAPTER ONE:

Your video strategy sucks… Deal with it

CHAPTER TWO:

Top ten reasons why your video campaigns fail

CHAPTER THREE:

Say it with me… Understand your audience!

CHAPTER FOUR:

Effective visual content

CHAPTER FIVE:

The visual content ecosystem

CHAPTER SIX:

How to sell video to your boss

CHAPTER SEVEN:

Ideas vs budget

CONTENTS

CHAPTER EIGHT:

Quality vs expedience

CHAPTER NINE:

Video content calendar

CHAPTER TEN:

Developing effective visual content

CHAPTER ELEVEN:

Writing effective animation content

CHAPTER TWELVE:

Getting what you want… How to give feedback and get better content as a result

CHAPTER THIRTEEN:

Building a video marketing strategy

CHAPTER FOURTEEN:

The eight most popular and effective uses of video marketing

CHAPTER FIFTEEN:

Conclusion and final thoughts

INTRODUCTION

INTRODUCTION

About the author and this book

If you look me up on the internet (and I encourage you to do so if you haven't already because reading a book about the rise of the visual content agency that is filled with advice on how to be a visual content agency by someone you've never heard of is kind of weirdly unsettling) you will probably read the following:

As a creative leader with over 18 years of experience within the Film and Television industry, Thomas has enjoyed a long track record of consistently delivering on time and budget high end creative solutions across all mediums, including TV, Film and all Digital channels (Web, Mobile, Social Etc.).

His work covers both creative and strategic thinking and he works with many of the worlds leading brands and creative agencies.

Here and throughout Southeast Asia, Australia, New Zealand and beyond - Thomas has worked with a pretty exciting list of local and international businesses, brands and agencies, including: Aegis Media Dentsu, APV, The Australian Government, BBH, Buchanan Group, BUPA, Burninghouse, Coca-Cola, Creativa Videos, Heinz, IXL Appliances, KAO, Kraft, Maille, Manulife, NRMA, PZ Cussons, Reckitt Benckiser, Red Bull, Rolls-Royce, Shangri-La Hotels, STW Group, Subway, Unilever and many more...

Having worked his way up the traditional film, TV and video industry path, he has an intimate and practical knowledge of all the production processes and how to leverage them for the best possible outcome.

This makes him an extremely reliable leader for any sized project as he can analyse quickly and solve efficiently any challenges that arise during the production process.

Furthermore, his experience with so many different forms of Visual Content from disposable captured content right through to long term, million dollar plus evergreen projects has helped him develop a unique perspective of responsibility and deep understanding of timelines and deadlines.

Essentially what all of this means is that in the cutthroat industry of visual content making and advertising I have not only survived longer than the average visual content maker I have actually prospered, thrived, progressed and had a career which still continues to this day.

How I have managed to do this is by continuing to deliver successful outcomes for the large volume of international clients that I work for, while simultaneously helping them to better understand their audience and what is required for them to deliver effective visual content that not only engages that audience but encourages them to take measurable action and delivers ROI for their business.

I can however only help so many clients directly a year and while I would like to help more I am limited by the amount of days in the year and the strict conditions I set myself for work that I really want to work on.

So in this my fourth book I have decided to create something for the clients I haven't had a chance to meet yet and share with them some of the fantastic insights I have developed over a life time making visual content that I know will help them better understand why their current video strategy isn't working and providing them with some of the essential tools to get their strategy back on track.

The best way to improve in anything you do is to spend time understanding what it is you are doing wrong and then taking the time to learn from this knowledge and applying it.

Not everyone can make great videos or develop a great video strategy for a business but I am certain that the knowledge in this book will enable you to better navigate the changing world of video production, create better more successful videos and animations and most of all…

Learn to better understand your audience because in the end that is what this is all about.

I hope you enjoy what I have to say and that you find this book useful.

Thomas Elliott

Hong Kong August 2018

CHAPTER ONE

CHAPTER ONE

Your video strategy sucks deal with it…

Despite outward appearances content marketing and video marketing actually have quite a lot in common with each other and you can indeed learn from what you do well in one and apply it to the other and vice versa.

This will help you start to develop a best practice scenario across both of these forms of marketing while also achieving a higher success rate in the outcomes you derive from them.

Content and video marketing both require an exceptional amount of deep rational and emotional thought as well as careful planning, an acute awareness and understanding of the target audience (of what they want and need and what you provide them), an understanding the "buyer's journey", a key business objective you want to achieve from the content and the message or messages (not to many) must be well crafted and executed.

The operative word when it comes to deploying either type of content is **strategy**.

Strategy is defined as:

strategy

ˈstratɪdʒi/

noun

noun: strategy; plural noun: strategies

1.

a plan of action designed to achieve a long-term or overall aim."time to develop a coherent economic strategy"

2.

the art of planning and directing overall military operations and movements in a war or battle."he was a genius when it came to military strategy"

Understanding strategy in content is important because content without strategy is just white noise.

Its a distraction that few will look at and even fewer will engage with and be motivated to action by.

From 2015 onwards most B2B and B2C companies have been starting to actually get serious about investing in content, so much so that almost 40% of their marketing budgets this year (2018) are now actively allocated towards content.

It's only recently however, that video has started to seriously become an essential component of content marketing strategy and spend.

Why has it taken so long to be added to the marketing mix?

The number one barrier for adding video is lack of defined and actionable **strategy**.

The second barrier by the way is still price - with many marketers failing to understand the value proposition in creating and distributing video on a regular basis.

I however see this second barrier as still deriving from the first barrier - the lack of **strategy** and strategic thinking.

If you talk to any marketer in any marketing department in the world most of them by now will tell you how they really understand that video is absolutely one of the best ways to help drive traffic, awareness, and conversion.

If you dig deeper though and ask them more about video and how they are using it across their brand it soon becomes very apparent that most of them lack the expertise, skill, and budget to pull off a strategic video plan aligned with their company goals, and at least 90% of them are yet to have the vaguest idea about how to figure out the ROI of their production investment.

Over the last ten years I have seen the conversation gradually shift across B2B and B2C organisations from marketing budgets that totally excluded video (except at the higher budget range where many companies exclusively produced television commercial content or higher level brand engagement campaigns designed for social and online) to companies wanting to produce at least one or two videos for their homepage, perhaps their social channels or for a big event or strategic objective for the year.

A lot of this content tends to be things like a testimonial, an "about us" or a company culture or recruitment drive video.

It seems like this is where video production most often comes to a halt; producing one video.

The question I ask time and time again is "how can you produce ONE solitary video, and hope it will lead to measurable results?"

Do you hang your marketing results on one written blog?

People used to talk about online video…

Why?

Because it was an easy term we could all bandy about that differentiated the kind of content you put online versus the kind of content you put on TV…

Often this content was differentiated by price - TV: big budget brand advertising…

Online: smaller budget more functional/rational content…

This price spend was also dictated by the assumed size of the viewing audience (TV: big audience… Online: who knew) …

But now we just talk about content…

Why?

Because the exponential growth of video across the spectrum of viewing devices (TV, Mobile, Online, Social, OOH, Cinema etc.) has fundamentally changed the viewing habits of the audience.

They don't think about online video anymore…

Just like they don't differentiate streaming services like Netflix from TV or Cinema…

It's just another option where they can watch what they want to watch when they want to watch it…

So why are so many advertisers, brands and businesses approaching their visual content as if its TV with one-off campaigns and activity targeted around major events in their calendar?

When what they should be doing is thinking like regular content producers.

TV and magazines have been thinking this way for a while…

Some brands are starting to catch on, and if your, agency, brand, business or organisation is smart it will too.

Stop thinking about the campaign and start thinking about content and more importantly start thinking about content at scale…

Because video demand is growing daily and if you want your audience to know about you and what you are doing (and not what your competitor is doing) …

You need to feed that need.

I know what you're thinking right now…

"Yeah I hear you Thomas, but what you just don't understand is that video is expensive" …

My response "Well that's because you are still thinking in terms of one video at a time… Often for one specific need".

Yes, video for a one-off campaign can be expensive…

Every time you need to pull out the cameras for a shoot, every time you need to add more craft with more crew and expertise, there is a cost involved.

So why aren't you thinking about maximising those times by planning and thinking about all the other opportunities that can be designed, crafted and captured every time you put together a video?

For example, if you are shooting something as simple as a talking head interview video – can you capture some frequently asked questions content with the person being interviewed?

Can you shoot content that you park and use at a later date?

More is more…

When you are producing animation…

Why aren't you thinking about the other opportunities that can be leveraged from the assets you've already created?

You've paid for them to be designed…

Why shouldn't you do more with them?

Can you make another video out of them?

Can you use the characters or assets in other collateral?

Then there is the question of craft…

Every video doesn't have to cost a fortune.

You need to match the customers' needs to the video content you're producing.

Many brands are already building out their content library by thinking about the steps I've outlined above for live action video and animation and where appropriate adding user generated content from their audience that speaks to their audience.

By producing and marketing more videos and using video analytics to track and measure the results of each video, you will also find that you now have the opportunity to measure which approaches worked best with your target demographics in terms of tipping your sales needle where you need it to be…

Without breaking the budget on each individual video launch.

The key to getting your content seen and acted upon is no longer about just having high-quality video – The key is that your content has a creative vision.

A well produced "about us" or "culture" video on your most trafficked page can not only provide a way for a prospect to connect with your brand immediately, it's also a fantastic way to impact a visitors "time on site", positively impacting your SEO.

One video, like having only one blog post, will always leave you feeling disappointed.

As we conclude this first chapter let's break things down a little further and gain a little more clarity…

As much as marketing and the content marketing space has changed, what has remained the same since the dawn of marketing (and will always remain the same no matter where the space evolves to next) is the need to connect with your target audience at the right time, in the right way, in the right place, with a relevant message targeted to a need they have that you can fulfil.

A one stop shop message doesn't and never will cut it.

So where do you begin to create a video marketing strategy, especially when you have a limited budget?

This is what we will unpack throughout your journey through this book.

CHAPTER TWO

CHAPTER TWO

Top ten reasons why your video campaigns fail

There are numerous reasons why a video campaign fails, in this chapter I will highlight for you ten of the most common reasons why your videos (whether they be user/self-generated or more polished internal and external video communications that are either live action or animation) fail or have failed.

Most of these mistakes can be easily avoided…

Like really easily…

Anyway, on the following page you will find common fail number one…

VIDEO FAIL NUMBER ONE:

Too Damn Long!

No matter what kind of visual content you have made be it a highly disposable piece of self-generated social content to celebrate world ninja day or a highly polished piece of enduring brand content...

If the video feels too long…

Then it's too long…

I know you want to give your viewers all the information you can, but there is a point and time where that amount of information begins to bore the viewers instead of intrigue them.

Expect the best response from your viewers when you keep your videos less than 2 minutes long.

If your message is longer than this here is a hot tip - try developing the content in a way that it can be broken into multiple videos that individually all have value to your audience.

By doing this you encourage the audience to engage with more of your videos and to digest the information in a way that is palatable and respectful of their time commitments and how interesting your story is to them.

If making LinkedIn Videos - keep your video to one clear message, under 90 seconds with a strong and clear call to action!

VIDEO FAIL NUMBER TWO:

Too Many Product Features Not Enough Customer Benefits!

So you've made an awesome product...

Well done you!

You know its awesome and you are pretty sure your customers are going to think so too...

So you want to tell them all about it through video!

Great idea...

Research shows product videos at the online point of purchase drive customer buying intent and make products feel more real to potential customers...

So why aren't your customers buying?

As awesome as your product's features may be, at the end of the day customers really just want to know what's in it for them.

Talking solely about product features throughout your video becomes meaningless and could do more harm than good.

So instead, use that time to show how those features could impact the customer and make their life better or easier...

VIDEO FAIL NUMBER THREE:

You Told The Audience

Too Much!

Obviously since you are the creator of your products or services (or the brand custodian at the very least) you know everything about them...

Some would say you are obsessed with knowing everything about them...

So naturally you feel the need to share that obsession with your audience.

You want them to know as much about the products or services as you do...

Then they can't help but love them also…

Right?

No…

Wrong…

You want to give your audience a taste of your products and services not a whole meal…

A snack…

If you show the audience everything what would be the point in them getting the product or service themselves?

Showing your audience everything can be too much.

Think of your video as a trailer; you want to persuade viewers to see the whole film, not give the whole film away.

VIDEO FAIL NUMBER FOUR:

Your Script Is Boring!

In order to have engaging and effective video, you need an interesting story to tell.

Without it, your audience will get bored and drop out well before its over.

There is no greater sin in script writing than what I term "Audible Print".

Sure you can say it out loud it has buzz words and something resembling a call to action but its not interesting, engaging or designed to work in the visual medium.

Effective Visual Content has a story and this story has a beginning, middle and end (though it doesn't always have to be in that order... See Kubrick's theory of non-submersible chunks)....

If you are just starting out with video try the following structure:

The beginning incorporates the problems that your product/service will solve for your audience.

The middle shows the audience the solution to the problems presented.

The end tells the audience how to use your product/service to solve their problem and how they can get it.

VIDEO FAIL NUMBER FIVE:

Too Much Voice Over!

This often results as an extension of fails one through to four.

Too much voice over syndrome comes from the idea that you need to jam as much information into your video as possible so that you solve everything for your audience…

And so you get the most value out of every single video you produce…

This is a mistake.

You need to remember that voiceover's purpose is to complement your video or animation...

Not tell us exactly what is happening visually at any one given moment...

A good video is a combination of visuals and sound.

When there is too much voiceover it ends up harming the story and the video or animation on screen.

In a one-minute video, you can usually get about 140 words in comfortably.

While that may not seem like enough to get all your points across, expert script or copywriters could easily help you tell your story in that amount of wording.

VIDEO FAIL NUMBER SIX:

Your Voice Over

Sounds Terrible!

Something overlooked in video and animation is the quality of the voice over (both in terms of recording quality and performance quality).

When doing your own voice over for your self generated content its important to use quality microphones for a professional sounding voiceover.

This makes a big difference in the outcome of your video's overall quality.

Using a more enthusiastic voice, doing several takes, & pronouncing your words clearly and correctly are just a few of the things that could go a long way when it comes to the nature of your video.

When it comes to videos from an agency or production company many people sacrifice quality for cost and go with a lower cost supplied voice over rather than paying more for a directed session in a studio with talent (usually for no other reason than they don't know what the benefit is in paying more).

A directed voice over allows you to get the voice over the way you want it with inflections in all the right places, pauses where you want and need them and a richer voice over experience than you can get from any supplied voice over.

VIDEO FAIL NUMBER SEVEN:

Your Stock Music Sucks!

Background music plays a highly important role in your video.

It is often one of the most powerful ways to support your visuals, drive the video forward and create emotion around your messaging.

So how come this isn't the case with your video?

Often its because you didn't spend the time and money to find the right piece of music for your video (and it is a combination of both of these factors... Don't underestimate how long it takes to find good music)...

You selected something corny...

Or you made the cheap music too loud in the edit.

Cheap stock music should be avoided at all costs…

Yes I know you can find royalty free tracks on the internet for $3…

I know they exist…

But do you really want a $3 track to support your new social video?

There is a reason the track costs $3…

Not only is the price cheap…

It sounds cheap too…

And cheap music with fake instruments doesn't help your video...

It takes your audience out of it...

So how do you select the right music for your content?

1. Start with feelings

How do you want your audience to feel when they watch your content?

Should they be excited or should they be on the verge of tears?

Picking the right tempo, style and instruments can have a big impact.

2. Avoid cheap sounding digital instruments

Nothing sounds more dated than synth instruments that are trying to replicate real ones.

If you want it to sound real...

Use tracks that use real instruments.

3. Be John Carpenter... Not John Williams

The John Carpenter philosophy is that music should be like carpet...

You put it down on the floor...

It supports your feet but after a while you don't even know it's there...

This works well for Visual Content.

4. If you can afford it get it composed

Composed music is in most instances better to stock and can be composed specifically for your content and can be a great identifier and differentiator for your brand.

VIDEO FAIL NUMBER EIGHT:

Your Animation Characters Are Poorly Designed!

This fail relates specifically to animation videos and particularly explainer animations which have become more popular for brands, businesses and organisations alike and like most of these fails it can be avoided.

Using characters in your animation video can be helpful in telling your story and making it relatable to your audience, but having badly detailed illustrations, poorly designed characters or all too obviously stock characters can rapidly reduce interest in your audience.

Using expert illustrators and designers is important in maintaining a good quality video.

No one likes to see poor animation (unless its intentionally poor for humour or to make a point) or faces not drawn properly, characters they have seen in a thousand other low cost animations etc.

Skilled drawers are always your best option.

Go with an agency or studio who have the resources to draw amazing and innovative characters for your video.

VIDEO FAIL NUMBER NINE:

Your Animations Lack Animation!

As I said before in an earlier point about their being too much voice over, animation alone can often not be enough...

Its not enough just to have a graphical representation of an idea or a cool character who doesn't do much more than stand there while narration and text supers happen around them...

Having dynamic movement on the screen is essential, and having enough movement is what keeps your audience engaged and watching.

No audience member wants to sit through a video that is mostly narration and barely anything happening on screen - this is what I would call an animated powerpoint presentation (and in most cases these end up being less engaging than a powerpoint presso because at least that has a real life human being you can connect with talking through the presso when the graphics get dull).

People want to watch your video, so make sure you give them something worth watching!

VIDEO FAIL NUMBER TEN:

No Call to Action!

When making a marketing or sales video you need to have a unique call to action at the end of your video that directs your audience to either make some form of contact with you or provides them with enough of a push to commit to making a sale with you.

You can't just leave out the call to action at the closing statement of your marketing or sales video and expect to get a lot of leads contacting you or any direct sales…

Yet this is a common mistake of a lot of marketing and sales videos…

They just end…

Or they end with a drive to a generic home page URL not one with information specific to what the audience is looking for.

You want to leave off on a note that will have customers waiting to see more from you.

Give them access to a custom landing page or use a trackable phone number so they have a way to contact you, and make sure to remind them why your product or service is for them!

Use this chapter as a benchmark when reviewing every single new brief, pitch, script, storyboard, final video you produce and you can avoid them in the future and your videos will already have a far greater chance of success.

CHAPTER THREE

CHAPTER THREE

Say it with me… Understand your audience!

One thing that I know for sure and that mountains of research conducted all over the world clearly shows is that communicators who understand their audience are more successful in achieving their communication goals.

Video is a medium for communication.

For it to be effective it is essential that the content understands the audience.

Understanding your audience can help you answer questions like:

- How much do they already know about my brand, products or services?

- What do they think about my brand, products or services?

- What are their goals?

- How does my brand, product or service help them achieve those goals?

- How can I tie a business objective to those goals and communicate this to my audience?

The following guidelines are the fundamental basics that I use when talking to clients initially about their audience and will help you understand your audience and help you achieve the results you want.

They are a good place to start but you should evolve these over time as your audience understanding deepens.

Step One: Identify your audience

In some cases, you may already be familiar with your audience, such as a customer you've already engaged with in store or on social media for many years or your product has a clearly defined and delineated target audience (it is for instance a toy product for outgoing boys aimed five to nine).

In others, you may be encountering one with whom you are much less familiar, such as the media, a new customer for a new product launch, a government agency etc.

If you are not familiar with your audience, making an informal list of the kinds of people who comprise it can help you approach the research necessary to understand them.

Be as specific as possible.

There is no content that is designed for all audiences as much as people like to think there is.

Even with wide appeal content there is still a core target audience in mind.

Step Two: Analyse your audience

To optimise your communication, you will need to know not only who your audience is, but also what they need from your communication task.

People in other fields aside from your own, for instance, may have specialised knowledge, but may not understand anything of value in your area of expertise.

They will need to provide them with some background information.

Your boss, on the other hand, has some understanding of your topic, and is most interested in the nature of your work.

She or he primarily wants to hear progress or results.

Regardless of your level of knowledge about your audience, audience analysis will help you gain such insight.

Step Three: Research

You can approach your audience analysis informally.

To understand your identified audience, start by gathering demographic and psychographic information.

Keep careful notes you can refer to as necessary.

Table 1: Definitions and examples of demographics and psychographics.

	Demographics	Psychographics
Definition	Statistical data relating to the population and particular groups within it.	The study and classification of people according to their interests, activities, and opinions.
Examples	age education level gender income level geographic region cultural or ethnic background	attitudes beliefs values loyalties knowledge level lifestyle

You can use the following informal research methods to find this kind of information.

Be sure to keep careful notes to reference later.

Review existing research: Conduct an assessment of any previous research your brand, business or organisation has done on your target audience (even if it is for content marketing versus research on video) you can also conduct a thorough online search to find studies about your target audience.

Brainstorming: Use your personal experience to think about the characteristics your audience might have.

Speak with members of your target audience directly via brainstorming focus groups or indirectly via brainstorming surveys and social media to expand that list of characteristics.

One on One Interviews: If you have access to members of your audience, talk to them about their background, beliefs, values, etc.

Record this as it is useful to transcribe and as a reference for all your future planning.

Step Four: Formulate conclusions about your audience

Use your notes obtained from your research to write easy to use and understand summaries of your audience and their needs.

Having a summary in writing will be useful to you and any other stakeholders as you develop your communication plan.

Its also useful to provide with any external agencies you may work with in developing and executing your content.

Step Five: Verify your conclusions

Verify your conclusions in order to make adjustments where necessary.

Consult a colleague familiar with your work who has experience communicating with similar audiences, or talk again with a representative of your audience.

Your stakeholders, co-authors, or your boss may also be able to verify your conclusions.

With a thorough, studied understanding of your audience, you will be better prepared to communicate effectively with them to gain your desired results.

From here you can develop audience profiles, their customer journey, content journey, target identities and so forth and so on that will again help you communicate about your audience to others which is essential when developing effective content for them.

CHAPTER FOUR

CHAPTER FOUR

Effective visual content

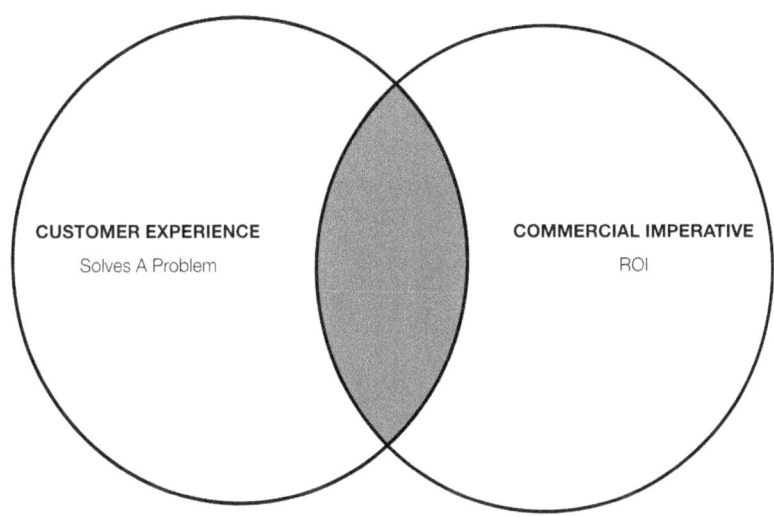

An essential part of creating content that delivers ROI for your business is understanding what actually makes effective visual content.

Further to this you also need to be able to communicate this quickly and succinctly to your boss and internal customers/colleagues so that they understand it and begin using this terminology internally with their teams (this helps make future internal sales substantially easier for you and by educating your organisation you are in turn educating their internal ecosystem and shifting their thinking away from one piece of content to thinking about the entire scope and scale of their content and how it interacts and engages with the audience).

I often refer to a version of the diagram on the previous page when explaining effective visual content to new clients who have never made or produced video content - or who have but have found that the content was ineffective or didn't yield the result they wanted.

My pitch on what effective visual content is goes something like this:

Effective visual content for a brand, business or organisation is always determined by how closely the content produced meets a specific customer experience or audience objective (it solves a need for them) while aligning with, communicating and reaching a specific commercial objective for that brand, business or organisation that solves that need.

You can not create effective visual content in a vacuum.

You need to understand the audience and what they want and match this to what the brand is providing in a way which achieves a measurable end result.

To develop effective visual content for a brand it becomes critical to target and identify with the brand as early as possible who the specific audience is for the video.

Many brands will tell you their audience is everyone...

But this is quite frankly more often than not either rubbish or just laziness.

Yes it is possible to create content for a wide audience but for it to be truly effective you need to understand within that wide audience who are the key demographics that you are targeting.

If its a sports drink for instance - are you targeting already existing users of the product? Are you alerting these users to a new variation or a change in the product?

Or are you trying to attract new users to trial the product for the first time?

All of these audiences require a different approach and the brands commercial imperative for these stories will also be different.

You can the allow room for some more generic broad messages (catch alls as I like to call them) that will appear to the casual viewer but you have ensured that you have reached the specific targets of the campaign.

Another important ingredient in developing effective visual content is your ability to measure the success of that content once it was released.

If you can show the effectiveness of the content by how many views, shares, likes, comments and purchases or enquiries it drove then it is a much easier to sell in internally next time you want to or need to make content.

CHAPTER FIVE

CHAPTER FIVE

The visual content ecosystem

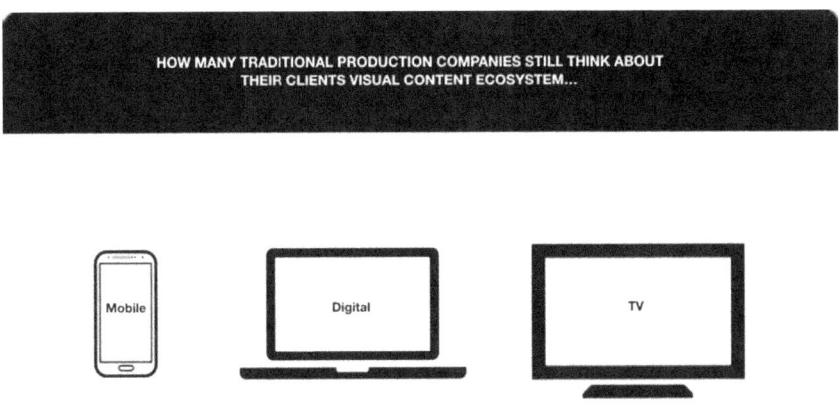

The visual content ecosystem is one of the most important tools that I use on a daily basis to demonstrate to my clients how I understand not only their content needs but also the lifecycle of each piece of content within their ecosystem and how much an individual client should spend to create, nurture and phase out that piece of content from their ecosystem.

Before we can get to that we need to understand what the visual content ecosystem is.

An ecosystem is defined as a community of interacting organisms and their physical environment.

A visual content ecosystem for a brand is a community of interacting visual content assets and the environment in which they live.

On the first page of this chapter you would have seen my grim graphic for how many traditional production companies (and indeed some clients) think of their clients (their own) ecosystem.

Often this thought is as simplistic as TV Commercials for TV, Brand Film for the website, maybe an Instagram or IGTV edit for social (which is really just putting one of the previously mentioned pieces of content on that platform with little to no consideration of whether it is fit for purpose for that platform or not).

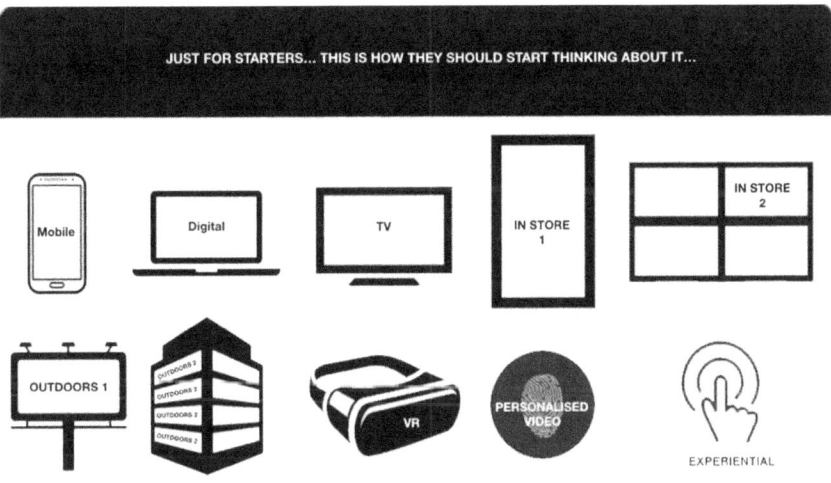

This graphic represents where your thinking should start when thinking about where your ecosystem lives…

Once you understand where the content lives you can start to organically think about the kind of content that should populate these environments and more importantly - how you create a feeling of seamless connectivity across all the content that lives in the ecosystem.

A great way to visualise this idea by yourself or with your team is to map your content ecosystem.

I do this in two ways.

The first way is to map the content which populates the ecosystem.

Just like any map four points of reference are required.

The first two points of reference relate to the content lifespan.

DISPOSABLE   ENDURING

The content lifespan is important for you to understand because you need to know that no piece of content lives forever.

It has a lifecycle and if managed correctly you will derive the maximum benefit from each piece of content in your ecosystem.

The first point of reference is disposable.

Its where all the content with a short life span lives in the ecosystem.

It is important to understand here that just because a piece of content is disposable doesn't mean that it has less value or is of less meaning in the scheme of the ecosystem.

Many pieces of high value content are disposable.

Most social video is disposable because it is consumed by the audience very quickly and then the audience moves on to the next thing that interests them on the particular social media platform the content appears on.

A lot of sales orientated content is disposable because there is a specific sales cycle and once it is over…

The content has no context or meaning to the audience.

The second point of reference I use is called enduring.

Some people refer to this point as evergreen.

I don't because personally I feel the term evergreen suggests that the content lives on and on and often places a false or misleading assumption with clients that evergreen content never needs to be replaced.

This is an amateurish way of thinking about a content lifecycle.

Every piece of content in the ecosystem needs to be allowed to die eventually…

Yes just like in life this might be sad but it is a reality of the shifting need of the audience which must be met at all costs for a brand to stay relevant.

Enduring content by is nature is the content that endures beyond a standard content lifecycle (which by todays standards means it lasts longer that twelve to twenty four months).

It is content that will still have relevance and in some cases if perfectly executed will grow in relevance to the audience beyond the standard content lifecycle.

The types of content that populate this section of the ecosystem are Brand Films, Testimonials, some Corporate Videos and Training Films that are not based on specific software or processes that are reviewed annually.

TV Commercials live somewhere between disposable and enduring depending on their message, target audience and how effective they are.

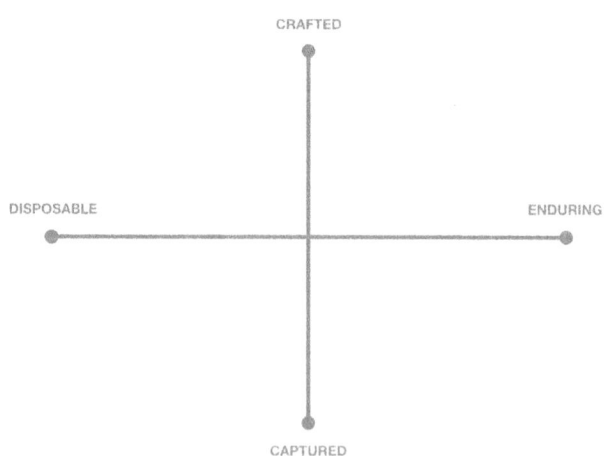

The remaining two points for mapping the content of the ecosystem are the points which relate to the production quality required for the content to effectively reach its target audience.

Its important to understand and accept that not every piece of content needs to be a polished, high production value, massive crew and cast extravaganza to reach the audience effectively.

In fact for some campaigns this approach is completely wrong (this will become clearer as I explain these two points).

The bottom reference point on our map is now titled captured.

Captured content refers to campaigns like the ice bucket challenge which are user generated content captured directly on a phone, camera or laptop camera and uploaded or streamed directly to the audience often without editing, colour grading, titles or any of the other elements that add production value to a piece of content.

Captured content can be (as was the case with the ice bucket challenge) as effective as the most piece of crafted content if it has the right message and approach to appeal to the specific audience.

It is also appropriate for many forms of internal video communication and some forms of hygiene content where a brand wants the content to feel like it is real, genuine, unedited, unfiltered and direct for audience consumption as is.

The last point on our content map is titled crafted.

I use the term crafted because craft more than anything else is a contributing factor in cost for a client.

The way I often position this to a client is to get them to think about the end credits of any film they have ever seen at the cinema.

On a big multi million dollar summer blockbuster where you are waiting for a post credit scene… You could be waiting a long time because of all the end titles featuring the crews names.

When seeing these names what you don't appreciate or understand is that each of those names has added their craft to the film.

Their specific or unique skill which has enabled the film to look as amazing as it does.

Like a lot of things in life the more craft that is added (the more crew the more expertise) the more expensive a piece of content can become.

Often when I communicate this to clients for the first time it is an interesting experience.

It as if the impenetrable unseen factors involved in project costs has suddenly become crystal clear.

Now that you have the four points on this first map the exercise becomes interesting for yourself and your team.

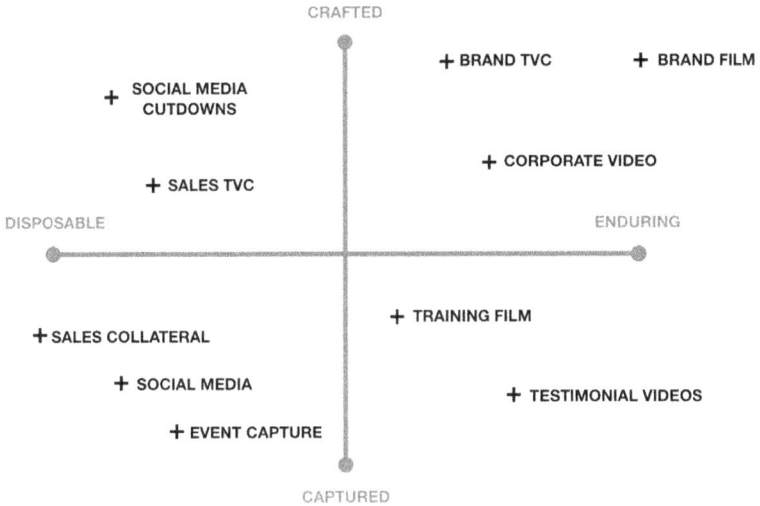

Using the four points of the map you can start to place your current content as well as the future content you need to properly populate your visual content ecosystem.

More than this you have also communicated this in a way which helps you and your team understand how each piece of content fits in regards to its longevity and an indication of how much each piece of content should cost by showing the craft that is required for each piece of content to be effective.

This is the first part of understanding your ecosystem.

The next step is to map this content against the environments in which they live.

This is also important because you start to develop an understanding of which pieces of content may migrate across numerous distribution channels and which will be single channel.

You can also start to plan for how you make the single channel pieces of content still feel integrated and central to the entire visual content ecosystem you have created.

A simple way of doing this is often to create a table or excel with the different environments the content will live on in the clients ecosystem (mobile, laptop, tablet, TV, streaming, VR, OOH etc) and list the content that will live in each environment.

You can then easily cross reference what is multi and what is single platform and start to develop the content accordingly.

CHAPTER SIX

CHAPTER SIX

How To Sell Video To Your Boss

Every time I consult with a new client or make a new connection on LinkedIn some of the first messages and inMail I get are from people who want video but can't sell their boss on it and do I have any tips on how they can better sell video internally?

There is little point to having a video strategy if you can't sell it so I find this is an important strategic step that everyone wanting to make video needs to understand and develop the skills to achieve the right result.

When I get a message asking me how to sell video I could very well tell the individual to compile all the latest data on video marketing into a phenomenal powerpoint and grab a few minutes of their boss's time…

But that rarely works and they'd be no further along in their plans.

So here are some of my best tips:

- Connect your visual content plan to their marketing agenda not yours.

This way your pitch already fits into their vision which makes it harder to say no.

- Demonstrate how your visual content plan creates an effective ecosystem of content to capture your audience at every stage of their customer journey with your brand.

- Present how your video will be measured, tracked and benchmarked via analytics.

- Outline expected ROI and breakeven point.

Differentiate income generated from your visual content plan from other marketing strategies employed.

- Show how landing pages and embedded links specific to your video will help track your audience from views to purchases and beyond.

- Show relevant and interesting examples.

By following these easy straightforward steps you will soon find that you are better able to sell video in to your key stakeholders.

CHAPTER SEVEN

CHAPTER SEVEN

Idea vs budget

I was contacted via LinkedIn by a former client (who I like very much) as they were frustrated as their two preferred agency/production suppliers back in Australia were not giving them enough satisfying "creative ideas" for their content and they wanted a recommendation for another agency they could contact.

After reading a series of InMail messages from the client I patiently responded that finding another agency wasn't likely to solve their particular issue.

The client thankfully replied with the response I was goading them towards:

"Why?"

Knowing both the client and the two agencies they work with very well I knew that the root of the issue was unlikely to be with the two agencies (who were more than capable and had produced highly creative work for other brands and businesses) and more than likely stemmed from the client starting every single briefing conversation for a new project with the sentence "I'm not going to spend much on this idea" immediately followed by the maximum amount they will spend (which was more than often low).

Now I'm not suggesting its a bad idea to be fiscally responsible or to have a clear budget in mind but it does tend to somewhat limit your creative discussions if you are pre-capping every single creative conversation before its even started.

When it comes to creativity you have to focus all your energy on that creativity.

I suggested to the client that next time they brief either of the two agencies they should park the budget discussion till after the idea has been generated and is fermented enough for someone to fully cost out...

By switching from a financial first standpoint to being open to an ideas first approach I told them they would learn at least four new things for certain from their suppliers:

- Some ideas cost more than others.

- Some are worth paying for.

- Some can be scaled back to a budget.

- Some can't.

But if its creativity you want...

You have to let the ideas come first.

When thinking strategically about your visual content budget consult with your agency partner on an annual basis to work out how much video you could conceivably produce from this budget.

You will find that by considering the annual budget as a whole as opposed to individual projects you may actually be able to get more video for your budget.

Often what holds back an agency or video supplier in the relationship is that they are limited to the thinking of the single project.

Once you open up the doors to a years worth of content you will find that economies of scale can often be made and your production partner will be more open to suggesting ideas that can add value to each campaign and in turn generate for you more video opportunities to reach your audience.

CHAPTER EIGHT

CHAPTER 8

Quality vs expedience

More and more we live in an age where as clients you and your audience are constantly forced to battle between whether you want **quality** or **expedience**.

Its a fact of life that more and more we want and expect things faster and technology and the increased productivity and simplification of processes that it has facilitated have more substantially amplified this demand satiating our generally poor impulse control and delivering us more of what we want, when we want it.

But have you ever stopped to ask yourself for a second if this is such a good thing?

Whether by giving in so readily to the idea of delivering a compromised product faster and cheaper than any competitor we are in effect increasing the acceptance and endorsement of mediocrity as a suitable standard that everyone should readily aspire to?

There should be a recognisable difference between creating healthy competition, disruption and streamlined competitive services versus creating a price driven race to the bottom that only ends in below average content delivered to clients that devaluates their brand with their audience and will increasingly deliver nothing more than lower and lower ROI.

Its also a fact that many clients see video only in economic outlay terms.

They do not or have not been persuasively shown that their video content is actually an investment and like any investment should and is readily capable of proving it can generate a reasonable return on investment (ROI).

So in the hopes of decreasing the cost of their video they are persuaded to look at production methodologies outside of the mainstream, hoping that as with many other forms of automation and digital transformation their is a quicker and easier way to create effective, measurable video content that connects with their audience and that with the lower price entry point is substantially easier for them to prove the return on investment to their peers.

This thinking more often than not has gotten many clients into deeper trouble than they were in originally.

Not because the thinking itself is inherently flawed (it isn't) but its just that the suppliers working in the space that deliver cloud based video solutions are not their yet in really offering a creative solution that understands and connects to audiences - it is at best video as a product, it is no where near video as a solution.

The other alternative of bringing production in-house is also more often than not designed to fail from the outset.

Why?

Well for the simple reason that most businesses are cheap when planing for this kind of capability and as such they end up with resources that are unable to meet all of their needs.

They usually end up with lower to middle of the range production and post-production equipment that is barely serviceable and the talent they recruit is of the lower end in terms of knowledge, skills and creativity (more often than not when a job is advertised for such a position it is targeted at a recent graduate under the assumption that at a lower price point they will add more value - but the question must be asked: "How much value can they add when they haven't really learned anything yet?, universities and film schools teach very little about audiences, demographics, brand and corporate communications, so a graduate really can't help you).

So with either the cloud based video solution or the internal team option you are really only progressing with limited options that can deliver limited outcomes.

Either of these two solutions only works for generating hygiene and hub content.

It fails at creating anything for brand and it fails at creating campaigns that will captivate your audience and drive them to take action.

An impartial third party will always be the superior option in providing this to a client.

They are able to be objective, measured and have more often than not recruited highly skilled talent from the top of the tree (while also grooming talent from the bottom up) so they are able to provide you with the best possible quality outcome for each and every video or animation you produce.

With every piece of new work you should ask yourself two questions:

If this was the only piece of work you had to show people would you accept the standard of the work as a demonstration of your skills and potential?

Would you accept others judging you by that standard?

If the answer to either question is no…

Then you know already that I have proved my point.

CHAPTER NINE

CHAPTER NINE

Video content calendar

We should all know by now that its super important to plan our content.

And even though we know should know this…

We still find occasions where we look up at the calendar see a super important event and think shit I don't have any content prepared!

When you're writing a blog post or an article this can amount to a little bit of pressure as you sit yourself down and crank out the requisite blog post, article or social post…

But when it comes to producing a piece of Visual Content (video or animation) and you want that video to captivate, educate, entertain or inspire…

The last-minute rush rarely produces the quality desired…

So how do you solve this…

Planning…

Sounds boring I know…

Its the kind of advice a parent gives and as I am writing this I can feel you rolling your eyes and shrugging at me.

But when you consider how much time goes into your broader marketing plan every single year and then consider the importance of the growth of visual content in said marketing plan maybe you should try preparing an updatable video content calendar…

You can do this with google calendar or your outlook calendar and I encourage you to initially make this a shareable calendar with your team (as they will often think of events you may have overlooked or have different perspectives on what content may resonate with a particular audience that the event is targeting).

You should start with the easy stuff - annual events, holidays, etc (these can often be filled in annually)…

Then move on to stuff you may want to change from month to month (product releases, updates etc).

Before you know it you'll feel better organised with your content and the quality of your content will go up too…

You can also share this plan with your agency or production partner as a great way to get them thinking about an idea for your content before you have even briefed them.

If they are a decent proactive visual content or video agency they will seize this opportunity and start to show you the value they can offer as a partner not just a supplier.

CHAPTER TEN

CHAPTER TEN

Developing effective visual content

Did you know that the average development time for a Hollywood movie is nine years?

Nine years and there is no guarantee that all of the films that go through this process are ever guaranteed to end up on the big (or small screen) in front of an audience.

I can sense already that the cynical amongst us are already thinking...

"That's exactly what is wrong with Hollywood" but before you get to that it's worth contemplating that the budgets of many of these films (once marketing is factored in) easily exceed the 100 million dollar mark (the average blockbuster now can cost well over 200 million) and the required ROI from the global box office grows higher every year.

So, what are Hollywood executives doing during these nine years to ensure they get that ROI at the end of the process?

They are getting to know audience demographics, their wants and needs and tailoring their product to meet what their audience wants…

And when they get it right…

They get it right big time.

I'm not saying that you need to spend nine years planning your visual content…

Your market changes to fast for that…

But just as with Hollywood, understanding your audience guarantees you a better result every time and to do this your project development time must be sufficient and the roadmap that comes out of it – your script must take you and your audience on the right journey.

Because most clients don't think highly strategically about video and animation (visual content) they lock themselves into the campaign mentality and campaigns always come with deadlines…

Deadlines that are more often than not too tight, unrealistic and don't leave a lot of breathing space for creative development.

Switching up your thinking from campaign thinking to strategic year long video as a communication channel thinking is the first step in breaking this cycle.

At this level you are able to think about the big communication pieces for the year:

- Brand Film

- Corporate Videos

- AGM Conference Video Content

- Holiday Messaging

- Recruitment Film

And the list goes on…

And you can start thinking about them early outside of the pressure cooker of a campaign style deadline.

You can spend time thinking about the audience for each of those videos.

What the audience wants.

What the audience needs.

What you can give each audience that fills those wants and needs.

You can in a word start being - **strategic**.

Sure there will be times throughout the year where you will still suddenly have to put out an urgent unexpected video to address a challenge in the marketplace or to communicate a change or some good news…

But without the pressure of all your other campaigns being run this way these campaigns become a fun challenge rather than an ominous task that you dread.

Try to get a brief out as early as possible for a project and give your visual content team (whether they are an agency, production company or in-house resource) time to respond with the treatment.

Once you have considered and approved the treatment, likewise spend time developing your roadmap for that project - **The Script**.

By spending time at the start getting these elements how you want them (rather than how you can get them), you will find that the content that is generated is super on brief, super targeted to your audience and vastly more effective at generating you that much wanted and deserved ROI.

The hardest step is changing your approach to video and breaking the campaign driven habit!

CHAPTER ELEVEN

CHAPTER ELEVEN

Writing effective animation content

I meet a lot of writers for writing visual content…

Like many people in the freelance part of our industry if asked "Can you write animation content?" they naturally almost always say "Yes… Of course I can… Do it all the time… No problem".

But the sad fact is…

Most of the writers I meet can't really write animation.

So what is so different about writing for animation?

I mean just like live action scripts you come up with a concept, describe the basic beginning, middle and end of the story…

You maybe then do an outline and finally you write a script…

Sounds pretty similar so far…

But it's the small differences that have a big impact on the overall success of the script…

Animation is in many ways a much more uniquely visual medium than live action.

Most live action scripts can describe the action of a scene in a few words…

For example:

Man walks into bar…

Falls over…

From here the director takes the script and with their cinematographer and the rest of the production team works out how to interpret this description and how to best cover the sequence to make the visuals exciting and interesting for the audience...

So how would the same scene look in a good animation script:

The man runs hurriedly along the busy street, his legs wobble like jelly as his feet occasionally get stuck as they drag along the sticky concrete, sweat pours from his face like a dripping tap.

He pushes passed busy shops, pedestrians and a man dressed in a hotdog costume standing out the front of a hotdog stand...

A customer at the hotdog stand squirts some sauce onto their recently purchased hotdog and it flies in slow motion across screen and lands square in the running mans eyes…

He swivels quickly and tries to swat away the sauce as he stumbles clumsily straight into a bar…

He turns and looks at the camera with a loud 'gulp' as three small birds and a series of lines circle his head, he drops like a rock, his neck stretched like a rubber band about to be flicked as his head tries desperately to catch up…

He drops onto the pavement as a cloud of dust flies up and engulfs the hot dog stand as the customer chokes through the dust and then bites into his freshly sauced hotdog…

As you can see the description is somewhat more comprehensive…

But it gives the animation team a much more complete visual image with much less need for interpretation.

Why is all this description so important?

Each character, prop, set in a sequence in an animation needs to be conceived, illustrated, then each sequence is style framed, storyboarded, laid out and finally animated.

For this to be done effectively both in terms of clarity of story telling and financial cost the animation team needs to know exactly the story they are telling visually and this requires more description to effectively and clearly communicate the visuals.

Does this mean animators don't improvise?

Of course not…

Every animator adds their own unique contribution to each and every frame…

But they still need a fairly specific guide of where the overall story is going in the first place and then they accommodate their flourishes into that structure.

So, any good animation script for visual content…

Particularly character based animation should have as much audio as is needed to tell the story and a lot of visual description that concisely summarises the action, gags and beats in such vivid detail that it leaps off the page, enabling the visual content agency, their client and the animation team to see the story clearly and know exactly how to execute it.

When planning your next animation campaign spend time developing the script and thinking about all the elements and actions you want to see.

By working this way at the script stage you will end up with a far more satisfying piece of animation that can and will achieve your objectives and that will also be a far more polished and engaging piece of content.

CHAPTER TWELVE

CHAPTER TWELVE

Getting what you want… How to give feedback and get better content as a result

Producing amazing visual content is not easy (amazing visual content agencies just make it look easy) and the workload can take its toll on everyone involved.

From having the right briefing and content development process right through to having the right creative, production and post-production teams to execute it and making sure that everyone from the agency to the client are all communicating clearly – there are a lot of things to get right!

One of the most important processes in getting the final piece of visual content you really want is giving effective and relevant feedback.

Whenever I start at a new agency or production company and start surveying their clients about the experience of working with them, a common frustration I often find is the clients satisfaction (or lack thereof) with the current creative and briefing process.

While clients often cite these two stages specifically what they are really highlighting is a lack of quality communication throughout the process that has led to what they now view as a compromised result.

Whether you are an internal client or an external client giving actionable feedback can sometimes seem like a challenge. Here are just a few of my tips on how you can give better creative feedback:

1. Start with something you do like

Doesn't matter how small or seemingly insignificant it is…

Pick something that is working and highlight that first.

Even in the worst video or animation, there is usually at least one thing worth salvaging and starting with a positive allows the feedback to start flowing.

Sometimes it can be difficult to see this clearly but everyone on your team is more often than not trying to do their best, they are putting in hard work (and even if it hasn't yielded the right result yet you have to trust in the process), and while you shouldn't have to worry about everyone else's ego…

Egos can easily get bruised…

And that just makes the process harder.

Finding one or more positives (more is always better), shows respect for the effort your creative, production and post-team have put into the project thus far by pointing out the elements of the project that work.

By putting a positive spin up front, you have set the stage to be more receptive when you have to deliver your feedback on what isn't working.

If you run into one of those rare circumstances where you find there is nothing good in the piece of content you've just seen…

Perhaps try leading off with acknowledging the time and effort put in so far before giving your honest critique and assessment of the failings.

2. Write your notes down and then schedule a feedback session

This might sound logical to most but it's amazing how often people get this one little step wrong and the wonder where the disaster came from later…

When you are going to give feedback - take the time to write down your feedback.

It doesn't have to be comprehensive even just the dot points but articulate it so you can articulate it clearly to others (tip: if it doesn't make sense to you… it doesn't make sense to others).

Booking the feedback session is also important - it lets everyone know that you have something to discuss and sets the stage that this feedback is an important part of the process.

Booking the session also allows everyone to mentally prepare and to be ready to listen and bring an open mind.

At the end of the session you should further summarise the discussion into a final feedback document which is distributed to everyone in the meeting so that everyone has a clear plan to move forward with.

Cold calling or dropping by someone's desk to give feedback can have disastrous effect for your project as in most cases – largely due to you being unprepared to give the feedback (as its off the cuff and unconsidered) and the other person is caught off guard and unprepared to take on the feedback (which often results in them being defensive).

3. Ask lots of questions and listen carefully to the responses

Before you criticise a decision, you need to know the intent behind it.

Without discovering the intent, you are more often than not only going to repeat problems or create new ones.

A good way to discover this intent is to ask a lot of questions.

Most creative work (from strategy to scriptwriting, directing, filming, animating, editing and so on) is often about making a creative choice.

This choice is often based on a series of different approaches the creative practitioner was presented with and in their mind, they have selected the right one.

Unpacking this choice is crucial to understanding a particular element or structure and why it does or doesn't work in the context of the completed work.

By asking questions you show both your respect for the team you are working with (and the creative process as a whole) but more importantly you keep an open mind and you may come to realise that the process selected once rationalised has added benefits that you had never considered.

4. Put action points in all your feedback…

Without specific issues to address you are at best only giving vague feedback that more often will require people to try and somehow read your mind.

Identify the specific qualities in the video or animation that your find problematic – its often easier to start with your high-level observations – "this call to action is too weak, we need something that drives people specifically to connect with us immediately, perhaps we drive them to call us?" … Before drilling down into more specific items "This font is too small" …

5. Try and give everyone feedback at the same time

Wherever possible try and give your team feedback at the same time.

Giving feedback to one team member and then to another increases the possibility of people seeing and interpreting your feedback differently.

By having a well organised single feedback session - chaired by one key team member who ensures that the feedback is understood and translated (even if multiple stakeholders are involved from both ends) it makes it substantially easier to build a consensus and generate action fast.

This enables you to keep your project on schedule without getting sidetracked by miscommunication which often leads to delays.

6. Follow up on your feedback

My final note is not to forget to follow up on your feedback. Even with all the steps above its important to ensure that everyone has a clear picture of what is required from your feedback.

Casually following up after a feedback session and asking a few more questions will help you quickly determine of the feedback is on track or if further follow up is required.

CHAPTER THIRTEEN

CHAPTER THIRTEEN

Building a video marketing strategy

Building a video marketing strategy is an essential piece of any successful marketing plan.

Whether you have attempted to create a plan before and failed or this is your first time preparing one, in this chapter I am going to help you learn how to use video to convert leads and customers.

I'm sure you're familiar with the marketing funnel, sometimes known as the buyer's journey or sales funnel.

In a snapshot, it's the steps your audience take from first recognising they have a problem to choosing your product or service to solve it.

Your audience need to hear the right things at the right stages of the funnel to move them towards sale.

You can use content to deliver those messages – it's a basic principle of content marketing.

Video as you know by now is such a flexible medium that different types of video content are more effective than others at various stages of the funnel and the customer journey.

Essentially, you can use video to take leads through their entire buyer's journey (solving their problems along the way and converting them from a prospect into a customer).

I call this strategic way of thinking about video – video content marketing.

Top of Funnel Content

To attract prospects initially, you'll need videos on high-level topics with mass appeal. Collateral in this stage needs to have an authentic tone, and aim to help viewers complete tasks that matter to them rather than push your products.

This could include:

How-to content libraries

Repurposed webinar content

Thought leadership interviews

Company culture content

Mid-Funnel Content

After using top-of-funnel content to guide your viewers to your website, you're now looking to help leads evaluate and justify your solution with more, in-depth or long-form content (the stuff you'll need the most of!).

This could include:

- Detailed product demos

- Client testimonials

- Video case studies

- Videos showcasing how your solution integrates with other key products and services in your customers' ecosystems

Content at the End of the Funnel

Videos can help you seal the deal when it comes to closing and they can help you post-purchase when you want to reinforce that you were the right choice.

Content in this stage can include:

- Nurture campaign videos

- FAQ videos

- Customer check-ins

- Instructional videos

Now lets break down further some of the goals you have around these types of content and how you can use them in your video marketing strategy to achieve your objectives for video.

1. Boost Landing Page Conversion (And Increase Engagement)

As you probably already know from other digital campaigns you have run, a good landing page is the foundation to a successful lead generation strategy.

In order to convert leads, it's essential that your landing pages communicate the value of your offer, establishes trust with the viewer and reduce any barriers your ideal audience might have about submitting the form.

While all these things can be accomplished with great copywriting, there is no better way to break down barriers than video.

Adding video to a landing page allows your audience to take in all the same information as text, but it also gives them a sense of your proficiency and trustworthiness in a way that words just can't.

Whenever we as a viewer are engaged with a highly effective piece of Visual Content (Video and Animation) there are several things going on in our brain that help us to tune in and stick with the content:

DOPAMINE:

When engaged in emotionally meaningful content, the brain releases dopamine which encourages curiosity and enhances memory.

In the brain, dopamine functions as a neurotransmitter—a chemical released by neurons (nerve cells) to send signals to other nerve cells. The brain includes several distinct dopamine pathways, one of which plays a major role in reward-motivated behaviour.

NEURAL COUPLING:

When the brain engages with video narrative its neurons fire in the same patterns as the speaker's brain…

Neuroscientist Uri Hasson has done years of research into the basis of human communication, and experiments from his lab at Princeton University reveal that even across different languages, our brains show similar activity, or become "aligned," when we hear the same idea or story.

This amazing neural mechanism allows us to transmit brain patterns, sharing memories and knowledge.

VISUAL AND AUDITORY CORTEX:

Video narratives stimulate the visual and auditory regions of the brain that process facts and engage memory.

The Visual Cortex occupies the posterior Occipital Lobe and is connected to the eyes via the optic nerve.

The Primary Visual Cortex (PVC) is highly specialised for processing information about static and moving objects and is excellent in pattern recognition.

The PVC contains a number of specialised regions that process things such as colour, spatial information, depth, texture and motion.

The Primary Auditory Cortex is located in the Temporal Lobe along the Superior Temporal Gyrus.

The Primary Auditory Cortex (PAC) performs the basics of hearing; pitch and volume.

It is important to note however that the perception of sound, as something that carries meaning (ie. Speech, music etc) does not take place in the PAC but through the processes of PAC in conjunction with other associated areas.

MIRRORING:

Mirror Neurons create coherence between a speaker's (in the case the video) and the brains of his/her audience members.

These neurons were actually first discovered in monkey's brains.

In humans, brain activity consistent with that of mirror neurons has been found in the premotor cortex, the supplementary motor area, the primary somatosensory cortex, and the inferior parietal cortex.

The mirror neuron system in the human brain.

Mirroring is believed to be the way in which the brain automatically interprets the actions, intentions and emotions of other people.

Mirror neurons, the cells in the brain that activate when we perform a particular action or watch someone else perform that same action, were up until recently only a theory.

Plus, video will encourage your visitors to stay engaged with your content and stay on your site longer.

As consumers, we just have a real hard time trying to skip past that super enticing play button.

You should also embed a short video above the fold on your landing page.

Don't forget to communicate the benefits they should expect to see and what problems your offer will help them solve.

Pro Tip: Plan out a series of short videos for your most prominent landing pages and record a series of videos for each one.

Make sure to do an A/B test of your landing pages to see how well they perform with video added.

2. Increase Webinar Registrations and Attendance

Webinars can be a great resource for people trying to learn something online.

However, they are a large investment of time, both for you to create and for your audience to watch.

Much like landing page videos, webinar promotion videos can showcase the webinar presenter and help the audience understand what valuable insights they might learn from the content.

Think of these videos like a network promo or a tease for a news story or radio segment.

They will work really well if you outline what you will be talking about but keep the reader guessing at what the answer might be.

Make sure to promise something of significant value to the audience and you are more likely to bring them along for the ride.

Try and use statements that will pique their interest and leave the audience wanting more.

Some examples that often work well are:

- You won't want to miss the number one tactic I use to increase conversions!

- Don't forget to stay to the end of the webinar to get a copy of our exclusive training resource.

- We'll reveal the results of our recent study on this topics, and I think you'll be surprised by the results.

Video has a unique way of hooking people into your story.

Think about how you can leverage the most interesting pieces to drive people to your events and to participate in your webinars.

Providing value beyond the webinar (such as pdf's and other learning materials) is a great way to capture your audiences details and to keep communicating with them once the webinar is over.

3. Utilise Lead Capture Forms from Your Video Player

Lead capture capability is not just for landing pages.

When you are ready for a video hosting platform, it might be wise to look at alternatives to YouTube.

As I have said many times before YouTube is terrible for lead capture as it is too distracting an environment for your audience.

While they may watch your entire video they are often distracted from conversion at the end of the video by another video (not from you… potentially from a competitor) that takes up their attention and by the time they have finished viewing that video they have forgotten about you all together.

One of the major benefits of other hosting platforms, like Wistia, Brightcove or Vidyard is that they have the ability to capture leads right in the video player.

This functionality allows you to gate a video at a certain point and require an email to continue.

So how can use this feature to drive new leads?

Have a webinar recording, video of a live presentation, product demo or case study video?

Allow your viewer to watch the first 15% of the video and then ask for an email to continue watching.

This tactic allows your watchers to get a flavour for your content before you ask for their information!

Usually between 30-60 seconds is the sweet spot for this kind of lead capture.

4. Explain and Showcase the Benefits of Your Products

Some products and services are just harder to understand.

If your website and social channels don't do a good job of explaining to visitors why they should care about what you have to offer, you could be losing leads (and revenue) like crazy.

Explainer videos are the perfect way to introduce new visitors to your business in quick, efficient and visual way that helps communicate how their lives could be better with your product.

As marketers and business owners, it's easy to get lost in our industry jargon and company-oriented terms. So don't underestimate the power of a simple, clear video that communicates value!

5. Help Your Sales Team Book More Demos and Appointments

Have you ever gotten one of those cold emails from a company trying to sell you on their great new product?

They "just need 10 minutes of your time," but they don't do anything to show you that they know about your company or your pain points.

Now, imagine instead that you get an email from that same salesperson, but instead of salesy text, you see a video screenshot that's showcasing your website's homepage.

Of course you have to click on the video, and when you watch it you find that the salesperson has recorded a really thoughtful video about your business and your website.

This is an amazing tactic that your sales team can use to connect with more prospects.

This kind of one-to-one video isn't going to go viral, but we don't always need viral content.

Sometimes we just need really **effective visual content.**

6. Social Media Videos

If you haven't noticed, video on social media is exploding on mobile devices all around the world.

In April 2016, Facebook changed the game by changing its video sharing platform to allow for autoplay where native videos start playing immediately as viewers scroll through their news feed.

This addition ignited users interest in video on the platform.

Driving more views, shares, likes and comments than ever before.

The addition of auto play has also ignited the video marketing world who understand that native video is now captivating viewing audiences at a pace 3 times more than a published video.

The number of Facebook videos views is by now well over 8 billion video views and is expected to dominate all social media published content across all social platforms for the next two to three years (unless other channels create an even more persuasive distribution channel for video - potential IGTV may do this).

Like all content on Facebook, your best bet to get your videos viewed will rely heavily on how much you want to invest in getting your content seen.

A promoted or boosted video will increase the likelihood that your video investment will get you directly in front of your targeted audience and give them front row seating to your content.

We know good content is key to engagement, and video tops the list for most shareable content on this platform.

Helpful Tip: Don't hesitate to try some different techniques when it comes to editing your video for social media discovery and distribution.

Consider using the first 15 seconds as a "tease" to hook your viewer and drive them to your website to watch the whole story.

The benefit to this strategy is getting the viewer to your website.

You can also break down existing videos into more byte sized snackable videos that your audience can consume more readily (this strategy also enables you to extend engagement with certain campaigns).

7. Middle of the funnel videos

These "consideration" videos are designed to move your viewer further along into the buyer's journey.

The content needs to be a little deeper and more informative.

During the consideration stage, you should aim to convert your visitors into leads, and inform them about your product and why it's the best option for them.

Your prospects are now considering different options, and looking for the solutions that will help them the most.

Of course, you want your prospects to choose your product over the competition's.

But this has to be an informed and well thought out decision.

You should ask yourself the following questions when thinking about content for this stage:

- What types of solutions do your buyers investigate?

- How do they measure the pros and cons of these solutions?

- How do they decide the solution that is best for them?

By continually answering these questions every time you are wanting to create middle of the funnel content, you will start to think like your prospects and can see if you understand their struggles, and if you are offering the best solution for them.

8. Product videos

Product videos are the ones that show your product in action.

You can use live action videos, or also a cartoon animated marketing video (to make it more engaging!).

9. Web page videos

It's time to get smart with your website content.

Everything digital can be measured so let's get measuring!

What are your most frequently visited website pages?

When your prospect gets there how easy is it to distill your message and hook them?

How long are your visitors staying on your most important pages?

Set a goal for next year.

Create 5 videos for your 5 most important website pages and analyse the results.

You can analyse your traffic, as well as your time on site which will ultimately impact your traffic.

The longer your audience stays on your site the better your SEO results will be.

Video is a key ingredient to make that happen.

10. Bottom of the Funnel Videos

These videos are designed to connect with your audience, typically your brand evangelists or ambassadors in deep and meaningful ways.

This is the last step before you close that sale, so your video content must be chosen wisely; you can't let them turn back now!

You should ask yourself the following questions when thinking about content for this stage:

- How are your prospects evaluating their options?

- What are the special features in your product that place it over any other one?

- Or what can they find in your product that might become a problem?

- Is there someone else that needs to be involved in the buying decision?

These questions have a clear goal:

You need to know the doubts your prospects still have, so you can learn how to address them.

The most important thing is trust.

You need to build brand trust with video content. You can do this by delivering the right videos.

11. Testimonial Videos

Typically these longer format videos are intended to be shared, and remind your audience why you matter and what you stand for.

These stories are educational at times, inspiring, thought provoking and when shared from a 3rd person perspective, are more authentic and less "salesy" than those videos told from a corporate point of view.

Helpful Hint: Testimonial videos often take more time to shoot, edit and produce.

Why?

Because telling a more in-depth story often requires using more characters (interviews), and locations, which adds to the cost of your shoot.

Get creative!

There are often opportunities to use an interview or part of your story to create a shorted "key message" video (s) to use for social media, web pages, etc.

Charlie Porter from Burninghouse a visual content agency in Melbourne Australia, called this kind of repurposing of content for further content creation - content clusters.

His theory is that content clusters recognise the content you create for external audiences, in and of itself present a unique opportunity for multiple content 'events' across your channels, extending the life cycle of your marketing beyond a single content execution.

Prior to the filming of a new piece of content, an announcement can be made on Twitter, WeChat, Weibo, Facebook or LinkedIn (depending on your audience) creating the expectation from your audience of an intended video shoot and fresh content.

On the shoot day itself you can create further engagement via social posts of on-set stills, gif's and video snippets that can be shared as Teasers, building upon the momentum of that initial expectation.

When the main content is published, you can work with your agency or team to create short promotional cut downs that can and should be released across all your social platforms, essentially acting as advertising for the audience to view the longer content, extending the reach and promotion of video - make sure you include links in the body description for the post or in the comments to drive your audience to view the main content.

Finally, once the main content has been released and has been consumed by its initial audience, a 'behind the scenes' video or a 'story behind' the video can further prolong your audience engagement and in some instances encourage your audience to re-engage with the initial content one more time.

This cluster approach is ultimately designed as an amplification strategy for your content efforts and should assist in bolstering your content calendar.

Video is no longer a marketing tactic of the future, it's here, it's effective, and it's measurable.

If you have a strategy, understand your business goals and what you want video to accomplish, and partner with a team experienced in getting results, you will find that it's one of the most cost-effective marketing tactics you can use because it can be leveraged in so many ways.

CHAPTER FOURTEEN

CHAPTER FOURTEEN

The eight most popular and effective uses of video marketing

Video is a terrific tool to help companies and brands accomplish their short- and long-term business objectives.

Whether your ultimate aim is to drive traffic, educate a current or potential customer, or share a glowing testimonial, video is the fastest and most engaging way you can possibly interact with your customers, short of a face-to-face conversation.

As you've already seen throughout this book there are so many uses for video across your funnel and the customer journey but here are eight of the most popular and effective uses of video marketing that you need to consider adding to your marketing mix.

1. Product videos

Product-centric videos focus on an innovative new product soon debuting or just released, where you have the keen ability to "show and tell."

You should use the product video to explain the complex features and benefits of your product (regardless of its complexity) in a simplified way that builds enthusiasm, highlights those benefits and demonstrates how the item works and most importantly how it integrates into the users life and lifestyle.

This should extend through the overall theme of the video (the through-line of the story) illustrating how your product intends to make the customer's life better.

Inspire viewers by painting a picture of a certain aspirational lifestyle and showing how your product can serve as the perfect accessory to achieve this lifestyle.

2. Corporate videos/Brand Films

Corporate videos and brand films are a great way to tell your new staff, partners, investors or customers who you are with a video that elevates your company's purpose and vision.

Using animation, graphics, on-camera talent or voice-over you can explain clearly and concisely with emotion and feeling what your company does, why you are different and what makes you great.

Use your corporate video or brand film on your website's home page, so that visitors (who are often time poor and don't want to read about you) can quickly understand your brand, your vision and how you can help them.

A corporate video may also be used to recruit the best talent on LinkedIn or other social networks, and to motivate investors and allies to seek you out.

3. TV commercials

Despite what you may have heard or read, whether international, national, regional or local, television is still king when it comes to getting a big brand message out to the masses.

Even in a short, 30-second or 15-second spot, there's a lot of room to experiment with and establish the creative expression and extension of your brand -- use emotion, fun, a "slice of life" scene format, a problem-solution approach, an informative spokesperson, etc., while presenting a well-crafted image that engages and drives retention of your brand and its overarching message in your audiences mind.

A great strategy can be to use targeted local advertisements to reach your local loyal customers, or national ads to grow your brand.

If your spot is strong enough and supported with a smart media buy, it can still put your company or product on the map or lift sales at times when sales are flat.

In some regions like Europe or Asia the TV Commercial is still an essential ingredient in any long term visual content strategy.

4. App videos

With an influx of application options hitting the Android and iPhone app stores every single hour of every single day of the year, the landscape for apps is super competitive.

Separate your company from the herd with a unique and memorable app video that displays its standout features and onboards potential users, even before the app hits the market.

Since app customers are hesitant to download an app without fully knowing what it does and how it works, a quick app video can go far to explain all the details to an interested party.

Excite your audience and show off the key features that make your app special to drive downloads.

If you are looking for a great example of how effective and persuasive an app video can be you should check out Sandwich Video.

Like many people who produce amazing and effective Visual Content…

They got into this by accident.

In 2009, Adam Lisagor made what became the first of many videos to come for neat tech products.

At the time, he was trying to promote an iOS app he had co-developed with a friend and decided that video was the perfect medium for doing this.

A year later…

Demand for his creative and video services had grown to the point where he incorporated as Sandwich Video Inc.

Sandwich doesn't just produce great videos and tv commercials for neat tech products and start-ups…

They produce some of the best video and tv commercials for neat tech products and start-ups.

Why?

Because they focus on product videos that have a human touch and rather than just focusing on the product or tech they predominantly focus on how the product or tech will integrate into people's everyday lives.

This works so well because it removes and demystifies the abstractness of a lot of cool tech videos and makes the product and tech seem instantly relatable, accessible and essential to the viewer.

In an article Wistia published on Sandwich Video with Sabrina Skau (one of the directors/creatives at Sandwich) the process of creating their videos takes about 8 weeks and comprises the following process:

- The creative phase: The team brainstorms ideas and writes a treatment.

- Adjusting the treatment: Sandwich works with the client to make sure they're hitting all the important points about their product and that the client feels good about the creative framing of the video.

- Scripting: Sandwich takes all the ideas from the treatment and puts them into a script.

- Pre-production: Sandwich finds a location and cast for the video, hires a crew, creates storyboards and photo boards, and selects the wardrobe and key set elements and props.

- Production: The actual shoot usually takes a day, although some require two days.

- Post-production: Sandwich edits together the spot, adds in VFX and motion graphics, colour corrects, and mixes the sound. This usually takes about a month.

This highlights another thing I really like about Sandwich… They make visual content (video and animation) seem achievable and the process pretty darn straightforward for their target market.

There is nothing complicated in the language…

No fancy wordsmithing…

There is what we do and how we do it…

And if this works for you…

Then great.

You can check them out at: www.sandwichvideo.com

5. Explainer animation videos

If you have something complex or new that needs to be explained, there is no better way to get your message across than with a visually powerful animated explainer video.

Using animation you can create locations, actors and props that are difficult or even impossible in the real world all on a laptop.

With the combination of audio voiceover and captivating graphics, you can demystify complex or multi-faceted topics much quicker than in a normal narrated video.

Animation is perfect for communicating simple messages, explaining a product or service and demonstrating complex processes that are hard to visualise or impossible to capture in a live action environment.

If an animation is well distributed on the right channels and targeted to the right audience, the return on investment could be invaluable long term and a typical explainer video can be turned around from concept to completion in around four to six weeks (depending on duration and complexity of the animation).

6. Website videos

Whether you are offering a service or a product or both, a video posted on your website is the fastest way for a customer to understand exactly what you are offering.

For e-commerce brands, a fun and engaging video can give the customer an accurate and intriguing glimpse of your product that he or she wouldn't normally be privy to without visiting a store.

With video living on your website, users should stay longer and interact more with your content.

The longer people stay on your website, the higher your conversion rate will end up being.

Website videos have one purpose and that is to quickly explain to a visitor what kind of product or service you are providing.

7. How to videos

Become a thought leader in your industry by creating easy to follow instructional videos.

How to videos are typically sought out by people in the industry and can often be found organically.

You can use them to explain how to best use your product, and promote ease of use, demonstrate features, overcome objections and to increase customer satisfaction.

Using a how to video you can quickly and easily explain the optimal way to interact with your business to set expectations high and raise current and future customers' (and potential partners') understanding of the ins and outs of working with you and your team.

8. Testimonial videos

We've talked about them before in the marketing strategy chapter but they are worth talking about again!

You probably know already that sometimes the best way to convince customers to buy your product or service is to show off the happy customers who are already using them!

Hearing a persuasive and convincing testimonial that shows expectation versus experience can be that final touch that helps you close the deal.

Testimonials can also be used to show off the features or aspects of your company or service that your customers love the most.

People tend to trust a testimonial more than a traditional video, since it comes from a third party and therefore feels more objective and "trusted".

Testimonials need to bring an authentic voice to the customer experience.

Again as I mentioned before using the EVE approach - expectation versus experience is often the best approach for a testimonial as it shows how another customer may have been apprehensive or unsure of your product or service or had wanted to know more but once they tried it and engaged with your brand or business they found that it was the perfect solution for them and their needs.

This enables your audience to relate to that customer story and to see their own journey and how the product or service could work for them.

CHAPTER FIFTEEN

CHAPTER FIFTEEN

Conclusion and final thoughts

Failure is not only an option…

It's essential.

If you've never failed (I never genuinely believe anyone who tells me that they always win by the way but for the point of my final chapter lets suspend disbelief) you've missed one of the most fundamental and beneficial life lessons you'll ever have…

A lesson you should have regularly…

In fact, I'd go as far as to suggest that we all experience failure every single day of our lives we just choose not to register it or accept it and we should.

I'm happy to admit that I fail at least one thing every single day…

Sometimes more than one…

Sometimes a lot more and I don't view this as a weakness and I am not ashamed to share this fact in my book.

Failure is the best teacher you will ever have and learning to respond and bounce back from your failures will prepare you much better for the next challenge that life is going to throw at you.

There is also no greater or more satisfying feeling than recovering from a failure…

Be it big or small…

Recovering from a failure builds confidence and makes us feel like we are suddenly on top of the world.

It makes us focused and enables us to see the positives in any situation again.

So if you tried video marketing the first time and you failed.

Thats okay.

Hopefully this book has taught you some valuable lessons for how you can improve in your video marketing and develop a better more succinct strategy next time so that you experience the kind of success you and your brand, business or organisation deserve.

Don't be afraid to ask for help either.

There are businesses right now in your city wherever you are in the world set up and designed to help you better understand your audience and how to devoted to helping you develop and execute an amazing video strategy.

So don't be afraid to fail…

Fail big…

Fail small…

Fail often…

Learn from your failures…

Repeat.

MORE INFORMATION

If you are looking for more information after reading this book please feel free to visit my website:

www.thomaselliottvisualcontent.com

I am available for workshops, conferences and one on one training sessions anywhere in the world.

NEW BOOKS

I will be releasing more new books via Amazon in the coming months.

Books currently available include:

Directing Visual Content

The Death Of The Traditional Production Company

The Rise Of The Visual Content Agency

Books currently in development and due for release soon:

Clowns who got lucky and other stories of working in content

If you'd like further information about these books please check my website or author profile on Amazon.